This book is to be returned on or before
the last date stamped below.

True Stories Of Edinburgh Castle

by Iain Gray

Lang**Syne**

PUBLISHING

WRITING *to* REMEMBER

Designed by Dorothy Meikle

Published by Lang Syne Publishers Ltd
Vineyard Business Centre, Pathhead, Midlothian EH37 5XP
Tel: 01875 321 203   Fax: 01875 321 233
Email: info@lang-syne.co.uk   www.langsyneshop.co.uk

Printed by Montgomery Litho, Glasgow

©Lang Syne Publishers Ltd. 2011

First published 1984. Reprinted 1985, 1986, 1987,
1988, 1989, 1990, 1994, 1995, 2003, 2006,
2007, 2010 and 2011.

ISBN 978-1-85217-149-0

True Stories Of Edinburgh Castle

A hill fort in prehistoric times and the site of a Roman camp in the first century AD. Edwin, a chief of Northumbria, established the first castle on the rock.

In the 11th century, Malcolm III, King of Scotland made the castle a Royal residence and began the task of uniting the country.

The 14th century - the Medieval castle proper - with David II's Tower (with flag) as the main defensive feature.

– – *through the centuries*

After the 1573 bombardment, the Castle had to be almost entirely rebuilt, and on the ruins of David's Tower - Morton caused the great defensive work to be constructed, known as the Half-Moon Battery.

After bombardment in 1573, the Castle had to be almost entirely rebuilt and the Half-Moon Battery replaced David's Tower.

The Castle in the early 18th Century - The initial attempts to build up the ground in front of the drawbridge are shown - the beginning of an esplanade.

The castle in the early 18th century and the beginnings of the Esplanade.

The esplanade, completed in early Victorian times, formed a parade ground - and now, also the stage for the Tattoo. The newest building, seen above the Half-Moon Battery, is the Scottish National War Memorial.

The Esplanade, completed in early Victorian times, formed a parade ground and now also the stage for the Tattoo.

The Black Dinner

The meeting place of the Scottish Parliament until 1639, the Banqueting Hall, or Great Hall, of Edinburgh Castle is now home to a magnificent collection of arms and armour, and also where the keys of the castle are proudly displayed.

Restored in the nineteenth century, its hammer-beam roof now looks down on the thousands of tourists who pass through it annually, but the roof and walls have also been silent witnesses to dark deeds that have shaped the very course of Scotland's turbulent history.

One of the most notorious of these deeds, known to posterity as the Black Dinner, occurred one dark and wintry night after the boy-king James II and a glittering retinue of courtiers and nobles had enjoyed a sumptuous feast in the hall in honour of the young Earl of Douglas.

It had been no ordinary feast, however, because treachery hung heavy in the air, and the festivities ended with the slaughter of the earl and his younger brother.

James II had been aged only six when, in 1437, he was enthroned as King of Scots following the brutal assassination of his father, James I, in a conspiracy orchestrated by some of his nobles.

Whoever controlled the king controlled the nation, and the young James became the object of a virtual tug-of-war between ambitious and powerful nobles.

At the forefront of this struggle to gain control over the monarch were Sir William Crichton and Sir Alexander Livingston, but they agreed to temporarily settle their rivalry when they became aware of a threat to their schemes.

This threat came in the form of the handsome and gallant William, Earl of Douglas, who had succeeded to his title following the death of his father in 1439.

As head of the branch of the mighty Douglas family known as the Black Douglases, the 17-year-old earl owned vast tracts of land in the southwest of Scotland, while another branch, the Red Douglases, held sway over vast territories in the northeast.

The family's power was so great that successive earls of Douglas appear to have considered themselves monarchs in their own right, and it was feared they were plotting to take over the ancient throne of Scotland itself.

The young Earl of Douglas did nothing to allay these fears, travelling about the country with a formidable retinue of 1,000 armed men and even disdaining to obey when summoned to take his place in the Scottish Parliament.

Whatever his true designs, his behaviour was to have fatal consequences when he accepted a flattering invitation from the king, at the behest of the scheming Crichton and Livingston, to come to Edinburgh to 'help in advising for the good of the realm.'

Ignoring advice from older and wiser heads that he may have been walking into a carefully prepared trap, the headstrong young earl, accompanied by his younger brother, David, accepted an invitation to dine with the king on what proved to be the fateful night of November 24, 1440.

A magnificent feast had been laid out in the Banqueting Hall, and the mood was jocular as the earl, flattered by the attention he was receiving, chatted easily with the young king.

The mood turned abruptly sour, however, when a stern-faced Crichton rose from his place at the banqueting table and in a thunderous voice accused the earl and the House of Douglas of disloyalty to the Crown.

While Crichton delivered his furious tirade, a servant entered the hall carrying a large platter on which a black bull's head rested in gruesome splendour.

A fearsome silence descended on the hall, as all were aware that the black bull's head, known as the 'black cap', was an ancient symbol of death, and signified doom.

The doom it signified was that of the earl and his brother, who quickly found themselves surrounded by heavily armed men, who seized and bound them.

A tearful James, shocked at the treacherous treatment of his guests that had been orchestrated without his knowledge by Crichton and Livingston, pleaded for mercy to be shown towards the brothers, but all he received from Crichton was the cold reply: 'Either you or they must die, for the kingdom of Scotland cannot hold both a Stuart and a Douglas.'

A summary trial was held and sentence of death passed on the brothers. Dragged from the hall, they were led out to the courtyard, where an execution block had already been set up, and beheaded one after the other.

Leap To Freedom

Rivals for the Scottish throne came not only in the form of powerful and ambitious nobles, but sometimes from within the royal family itself, and it is this that forms the basis of one of the most daring episodes in the castle's long history.

He may have been a man of learning, a gifted musician, a talented architect, and a brilliant conversationalist, but King James III was certainly not fitted for the role of the type of monarch that a late fifteenth century Scotland required.

Nothing less than an iron fist was needed to impose order on the realm and to resist English invasion, but the studious James ruled more with a velvet glove, favouring as advisors decidedly unwarlike subjects such as his shoemaker, fencing master, and court astrologer.

This understandably alarmed his nobles, and rumours reached the king's ears of how they planned to replace him on the throne with one of his younger brothers.

These brothers, Alexander, Duke of Albany, and John, Earl of Mar, although of the same Stuart blood, were made of much sterner stuff than their brother: Albany was a great horseman, while Mar was

A leap for freedom

renowned for his prowess as an archer, and neither were frightened of proving their mettle on the battlefield.

As the threat to his position increased, James took the step of having both brothers imprisoned. The Earl of Mar was confined to Craigmillar Castle, where he is said to have either died of a fever, or bled to death in a bath.

Whatever the cause of his untimely demise, it is more than likely that he was killed on the king's orders, and it is this that may have acted as a spur to the Duke of Albany to attempt to escape his own confinement.

By 1479 the Duke had found himself incarcerated in David's Tower, the massive and forbidding structure that then crowned the steep northeast side of the castle rock.

Aware that his life was in grave danger, he realised his only hope lay in escape. But how was he to achieve this near impossible task?

The answer came when he was granted permission to take delivery of two small barrels of wine that had been shipped to the nearby port of Leith: cunningly concealed in one of the barrels, as Albany had secretly arranged, was a length of stout rope.

The arrival of the rope could not have been more

timely, because a letter that was also delivered to him
warned that his captors planned to kill him the
following day.

Albany intended to use the rope to escape down
the steep face of the castle rock, but his four guards in
the tower would have to be dealt with first: he
cunningly, and murderously, achieved this by
inviting them to share his wine.

After quaffing several generous measures in front
of the great blaze that roared in the tower's fireplace,
the inebriated guards were easily overcome by
Albany and his faithful servant, who not only
brutally stabbed them to death, but also threw their
corpses onto the fire.

Leaving the sickening stench of the roasting
bodies behind them, Albany and his servant stole
from the tower to the battlements, where they
attached one of the ends of the rope.

The servant clambered down the rope first, but
catastrophe befell the escape attempt when the rope
proved too short and he plunged the remaining
distance down onto the rocks below.

The quick-witted Albany rushed back to the
tower and ripped up some bed sheets that he
hurriedly attached to the rope when he returned to
the battlements.

Firmly gripping the rope and pushing with his

feet against the walls, he leapt into the black night - the extra few feet of length proving sufficient for him to safely reach the ground, where he found his servant writhing in agony with a broken thighbone.

Albany could have left him lying there to his fate, but proving as loyal to his servant as the servant had been to him, he hoisted him on his shoulders and made his way through the night to the safety of a friend's nearby house.

After resting, he made for Leith, where the ship that had provided his wine and means of escape took him to his fortress of Dunbar Castle.

Albany was later reconciled for a time with his brother, but was forced to flee the country and seek exile in France, where he died in a tournament in 1485.

His brother, the king who had imprisoned him and forced him into making his daring escape from Edinburgh Castle, was mysteriously stabbed to death three years later after his defeat at the battle of Sauchieburn. ⋈

Death Of A Countess

The broad expanse of the esplanade of Edinburgh Castle is famous today as the venue for the international military tattoo, but in centuries past it served a much grimmer purpose.

Also known as the castle hill, it was the scene of a number of gruesome public executions, one of the most notorious and shameful of which was the burning to death in public of a beautiful young lady who had been wrongly and maliciously accused of conspiring to poison the king, James V.

What blinded James to the innocence of Lady Janet Douglas, the Countess of Glamis, was her connection to the House of Douglas.

The king had good cause to fear and loathe this powerful house, not least because the countess's brother, the Earl of Angus, head of the branch of the Douglases known as the Red Douglases, had held him in his power when he was a boy.

James's opportunity for vengeance against the Douglases came in 1528, when he reached the age of 17, and was able to rally enthusiastic support from other nobles to overthrow the family once and for all.

This vengeance was swift and merciless, with every leading Douglas either killed by order of the

Servants of Lady Glamis were tortured into making false allegations against her

king or forced to seek refuge across the border in England, and among those exiles who nursed their hatred of the king was the countess's brother.

The Lady Glamis, described by one contemporary as 'the most celebrated beauty of the nation', had been allowed to remain unmolested, but this situation changed shortly after her husband died and she later remarried Archibald Campbell of Skipnish.

In marrying Campbell, Lady Glamis had rejected the hand of her late husband's brother, William Lyon, and this was to have fatal consequences for her.

Furious at being rebuffed by the beautiful countess, Lyon fed the king's already implacable hatred of the Douglases by falsely accusing her of plotting with her brother against the king and attempting to poison him.

The countess soon found herself imprisoned in Edinburgh Castle, along with her husband, young son, and chaplain, and despite her protestations of innocence she was convicted of treason on the grounds that she had conspired against the king and attempted to poison him.

Much of the so-called evidence against her had been extracted under torture from her servants, and the general opinion at the time was that she was wholly innocent, with even the English governor at

Berwick writing to Henry VIII that he 'could perceive no substantial ground or proof of the matter.'

The proud countess had closed her defence to the court by defiantly stating that, 'It is the office of you judges to protect innocence from injury.

'But if the malice and power of my enemies be such, that whether guilty or innocent I must needs be condemned, I shall die cheerfully, having the testimony of a good conscience: and assure yourselves, you shall find it more easy to take away my life than to blast my reputation or to fix any real blot upon my memory.'

Perhaps ashamed of their conduct the judges, who had presided over what had been a mockery of a trial, timidly asked the king to show some clemency on her behalf, but this was coldly refused.

Under the harsh laws of the time, any female of rank who was found guilty of the ultimate crime of treason was sentenced to be burned at the stake, and this was the barbaric punishment meted out to the innocent Lady Glamis.

On the bright summer's day of July 17, 1537, she was allowed a brief and tearful farewell of her husband and young son before being led from the castle and onto the present-day esplanade.

The crowd that had gathered to witness her grim end were impressed by her calm and noble demeanour, as she was bound to a stake around which dozens of highly flammable tar barrels had been packed.

Contemporary reports state that the only sounds that could be heard as the oily flames enveloped her slim body were those of women sobbing and men cursing.

Either by chance or cruel design, the countess's husband had been able to witness his wife's death agonies: mad with grief, he made a desperate bid to escape later that night and fell to his death from the castle rock. ✖

Flames Of Martyrdom

It was not until 1560 that the religious revolution in Scotland known as the Reformation was finally recognised by parliament and the Presbyterian, or Protestant, faith was established as the nation's official religion.

For decades before that, however, and for a number of years afterwards, the country was embroiled in bitter and divisive civil wars that set monarchs against their subjects, fathers against sons, and neighbour against neighbour.

Every revolution requires its martyrs, and there was no shortage of these in the years immediately preceding the Reformation as numbers of Scottish churchmen began to question the age-old doctrines and practices of the Catholic Church.

Bloated with riches and power, the Church had gradually become estranged from its flock, and it was only a matter of time before the mighty edifice toppled.

It was not the fundamental Christian message of the Church that was at issue, but the manner in which many of its priests, bishops, archbishops and cardinals flagrantly flouted this message.

Among those who were uneasy with this

The Cardinal had an uncompromising reformer as well as a good man to deal with

departure from what they saw as the true preaching of the word of God was the young Scotsman Thomas Forret.

Forret had been destined for the Church from an early age, and while still a boy was sent to Cologne for his training. That period over, he returned to his native land, where a career of comfort and promise was ready waiting for him.

He was placed in the Abbey of St Colme, now a ruin on the island of Inchcolme, in the Firth of Forth, but at the time of his appointment it was in a full flood of prosperity and his future looked secure.

While in the abbey, however, he chanced upon the works of St Augustine, who had inspired the great German religious reformer Martin Luther, and he lost no time in attempting to spread this message among his fellow monks.

This upset the normally placid life of the abbey, and Forret was removed and appointed as the vicar to the nearby community of Dollar.

This failed to dampen his zeal, however, and the young monk embarked on what were then the unheard of and radical steps of reading sermons to his flock in their native tongue, rather than obscure Latin, drawing up a catechism of religious instruction for children, regularly visiting his parishioners, and carrying out numerous acts of charity.

Bird's eye view of
THE CASTLE of EDINBURGH

Also exhibition of history of __
Scotland's artillery __ and __
entrance to old prison vaults

Mons Meg

Royal Scot Museum

Palace Yard

The Great Hall

Scottish Regalia

Half-Moon Batte

Historic Apartments

Statue to __
Robert the Bruce
King of Scots
victor of Bannockburn

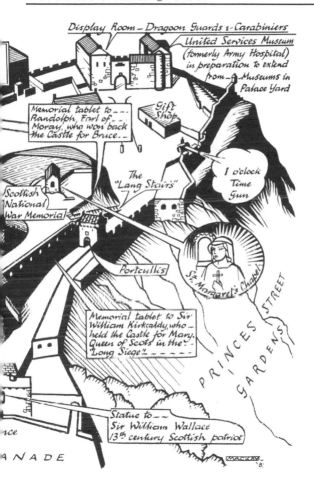

Display Room — Dragoon Guards & Carabiniers

United Services Museum
(formerly Army Hospital)
in preparation to extend
from — Museums in
Palace Yard

Memorial tablet to —
Randolph, Earl of
Moray, who won back
the Castle for Bruce —

Gift Shop

I o'clock Time Gun

The "Lang Stairs"

Scottish National War Memorial

Portcullis

St. Margaret's Chapel

PRINCES STREET GARDENS

Memorial tablet to Sir
William Kirkcaldy, who
held the Castle for Mary,
Queen of Scots in the
"Long Siege" —

Statue to —
Sir William Wallace
13th century Scottish patriot

ANADE

MACKAY '81

His activities inevitably attracted the attention of the Church authorities, and he was hauled before the Bishop of Dunkeld to answer for his behaviour.

This Forret did, and the bishop, admonishing him to adhere to established doctrine and practice, warned him that if he did not he would soon suffer.

This warning proved prophetic, when Forret was finally taken before the powerful Cardinal David Beaton and subjected to an intense interrogation.

Questioned by the cardinal on why he had read out the scriptures to his flock in their native tongue, the unrepentant monk retorted: 'Brother, my people are so rude and ignorant, they understand no Latin, so that my conscience moved me to pity their ignorance, which provoked me to learn them the words of their salvation in English.'

Furious at the monk's uncompromising stance, the cardinal declared him a heretic and that he must suffer the terrible fate of all heretics – to be burned at the stake.

As an example to others who might have entertained the same radical opinions as Forret, his execution took place on the present-day esplanade of Edinburgh Castle, in front of a huge and baying mob, on the last day of February 1539.

A Roman Catholic priest, Friar Arbuckle, tried to get Forret to recant his 'heresy' as he was tied to the

'Burn him! Burn him!' they cried

stake, but he resolutely refused. The doomed monk also tried to address the mob, but his attempts were drowned out as the chilling chant of 'Burn him! Burn him!' rang out.

Ironically, in later years, similar crowds would be baying for the blood of those adherents of the Catholic faith who fell foul of the stern authority of the Reformation.

As the acrid smoke rose from his funeral pyre and as the wind blew it across the esplanade in the direction of the present-day busy tourist thoroughfare of Princes Street, Forret was heard to utter the words of the fifty-first psalm: 'Have mercy on me, O Lord, according to thy loving kindness.'

A small degree of mercy was indeed shown, when someone knocked away the wooden block on which he had been placed, cutting short the last excruciating agonies of death by fire as he strangled on the rope that had been lopped around his neck and fixed to the top of the stake. ✂

Last Stand For The Queen

O nly six hours into the bitterly cold New Year morning of 1573, the citizens of Edinburgh were rudely awoken from their slumbers by a mighty explosion from one of the cannon mounted on the castle ramparts.

As they sleepily tumbled from their beds, the whole town seemed to shake as an earth-shattering volley of other guns tore the previously still morning air, and deadly cannonballs came whistling down from the heights of the castle and smashed into barricades that had been erected in the Lawnmarket.

This dawn chorus of artillery not only signalled that a brief truce between the castle garrison and the town had ended, but also marked the last stand in the doomed cause of the ill-starred Mary, Queen of Scots.

Five years had passed since Mary had fled into exile in England, and her cause had now been reduced to a small band of loyal subjects who held the castle in her name.

The siege of the castle had started in April of 1571 when Sir William Kirkcaldy of Grange and William Maitland of Lethington had tightly barred its forbidding gates and declared for the queen, and all subsequent attempts by her enemies to retake the citadel had ended in miserable failure.

The Earl of Morton, who had been appointed Regent, was now ruling Scotland in the name of the infant James VI, and his answer to the insolent thunder of the guns from the castle on that New Year morning was to intensify the siege.

To his great frustration, the castle proved virtually impregnable, but help arrived in March in the form of a great train of artillery that had been supplied to the Regent by England's Queen Elizabeth.

The queen had supplied the artillery, plus a force of infantry, to further her own complex political and dynastic interests, but it was gratefully received by the Regent.

Under the direction of the English commander, Sir William Drury, twenty of the great guns were strategically placed at key points around the castle.

Five were planted on the site of the present-day esplanade, five on the sight where Princes Street now runs, five more near the West Port, and five in Greyfriars Churchyard.

A final summons to surrender was sent to the castle, only to be answered with the hoisting of a red flag of defiance from David's Tower.

The guns began their furious assault on the

mighty bastion on May 17, and as the shot crashed against the walls of David's Tower a great shriek was heard from the women in the castle, indicating to the besiegers that they were not shooting in vain.

But the defenders were not idle: their ammunition was running low, but the famed Mons Meg and the many smaller guns mounted on the walls still managed to reply to the guns of the besiegers.

The heavier ordnance of the English gained the upper hand, however, when David's Tower came crashing to the ground in a heap of rubble on May 23.

The castle garrison realised they were doomed when, on the following day, their last defences of the Gate Tower, the Portcullis, and Wallace's Tower were all reduced to rubble under the incessant bombardment.

Other sections of the castle defences were also destroyed, and soon the entire fortifications were little more than a mass of ruins, leaving the castle open to assault by the waiting troops.

Realising the situation was hopeless, Kirkcaldy of Grange at last reluctantly agreed to surrender the castle, but not before obtaining an assurance from the English commander that he and the surviving members of the garrison would be taken into his custody, rather than into that of the vengeful Earl of Morton.

The commander agreed, but the English later reneged on the deal, and Kirkcaldy of Grange was handed over to Morton. Maitland had already died in prison, but a much grimmer fate awaited Kirkcaldy, who was hanged at the town cross on August 3.

His humiliation did not end with his death, for, following the barbaric custom of the time, his head was severed from his body and impaled for all to see on the walls of the very castle he had so nobly defended in the cause of his queen.

Mary's royal standard, that had flown proudly from the castle ramparts throughout the two long years of the siege, now lay torn in the rubble and dust, while she herself was destined to fall victim to the executioner's axe fourteen years later.

Burn, Witch, Burn!

One of the blackest stains on Scotland's historical record is that an estimated 4,000 innocent men and women were tortured and burned as witches in the period between the closing years of the sixteenth century and the final years of the following century.

All it took to be accused of the crime of witchcraft was the poisonous gossip of superstitious neighbours, and it was not a case of innocent until proven guilty but guilty until proven innocent.

Few, however, were ever found innocent, because horrific methods of torture were applied to extract a 'confession.'

These barbaric techniques included the thumbscrews, the twisting of a cord around the forehead, the shattering of the leg bones in a device known as the 'boots', pulling out the finger nails with pincers, or being forced to wear a hair shirt steeped in vinegar, so that the skin was pulled away from the body.

The hysteria over witchcraft increased to a new and frightening level in 1590, when James VI supervised both the torture and the trial of a number of men and women who were later burned at the

Folk were terrified of women reputed to be witches

stake in full view of the castle and the citizens of Edinburgh on the present-day esplanade.

The monarch, although academically gifted from an early age, was nevertheless no less prone to the superstitions of his age, and this was to have dire consequences for an innocent group of people now known to posterity as the witches of North Berwick.

James's fascination with witchcraft had a rather strange origin, springing from the difficulties that had surrounded his marriage to Princess Anne of Denmark.

The wedding was to have taken place in Scotland, but the ship bringing the young princess from her native land was forced to turn back because of a succession of extremely violent storms, and the impatient king sailed to Denmark for the wedding ceremony.

Accompanied by his new bride, he finally arrived back home to the port of Leith in May of 1590. He had not forgotten the storms that had threatened to thwart his marriage plans, however, and strongly suspected demonic forces had deliberately raised them.

'Proof' of this came when a young servant girl confessed under torture to being a witch, and named three other women and a John Fian, a schoolmaster, as also being in league with Satan.

They were immediately dragged before the king, who watched as they were all subjected to horrific torture in a bid to obtain confessions.

The torture of John Fian was particularly brutal: we are told how 'his nails were torn away with pincers, needles were thrust up to the head in his fingers, while his legs were crushed in the boots until the blood and marrow spouted forth.'

Tormented beyond all endurance by the agonies inflicted on their bodies, they all 'confessed' to having been in league with Satan, embellishing their confessions by telling of how they had met with the Devil himself at the church of North Berwick.

Their most shocking revelation, however, was that their main purpose in meeting with the Devil was to thwart the king's marriage plans and ultimately destroy him.

John Fian told the trembling king that when the witches knew the princess was sailing from Denmark, the whole company had gone out to sea, sailing through the air in sieves, and had raised the storm that had driven her royal vessel back to port.

One of the accused women, Agnes Simpson, confessed to a second attempt to destroy the king and his bride.

This occurred when the royal couple were only one day's sail away from Leith and, according to

King James was present at the torture sessions

Simpson, the witches 'had put to the sea that day and threw a cat into the water, pronouncing at the same time an invocation to the devil.

'This was intended to raise such a storm that the vessel would be wrecked and the king drowned.'

The king gravely confirmed this, as his vessel had indeed at that time been violently tossed about.

The fate of the accused was now sealed: in addition to the original five, a number of other innocent people were also implicated in the Devil's conspiracy to kill the king and most were burned to death at the stake on the castle esplanade throughout the early months of 1591.

It was not until nearly one hundred and fifty years later, in 1736, that Scotland's harsh laws against witchcraft were finally repealed: but superstition dies hard, and there are still many today who believe in a dark world of witchcraft!

Storming The Walls

Scotland had been in a state of political ferment ever since James VII had been forced into exile in France shortly before the accession to the throne in 1688 of William of Orange.

The unrest intensified in 1714 when George, the Elector of Hanover, controversially succeeded to the throne on the death of Queen Anne, and matters came to boiling point in September of the following year when the Earl of Mar raised the Standard of the Royal House of Stuart at Braemar.

Those who flocked to the Standard were known as Jacobites, and they immediately launched a military campaign to set James VIII, known as the Old Pretender, on what they believed to be his rightful place on the throne.

The authorities loyal to the Hanoverian government realised that Edinburgh Castle was of vital strategic importance and could not be allowed to fall into Jacobite hands, and ample provisions were accordingly stored in preparation for a long siege, while a volunteer movement was started and 400 citizens enrolled as soldiers.

The importance of the castle to the Jacobites could hardly be over-stated, not least because of the added strength and prestige it could lend to their cause, but also the rich spoils in arms and bullion stored within its walls.

A plan was devised to launch an assault on the citadel on the night of September 8, 1715, a daring scheme that came close to achieving success.

The plan had originated with Lord Drummond of Perth and a former officer of the Scots Fusilier Guards known as Ensign Arthur, who at one time had been quartered with his regiment in the castle and therefore knew its complex layout.

Forty of Drummond's own clansmen and another forty Jacobite sympathisers from Edinburgh were chosen for the risky enterprise, that was to be carried out under the leadership of the dashing Highlander, Drummond of Balhadie.

The spot chosen for the surprise attack was the northwest corner of the fortified walls, near the old sally port, while four members of the castle guard were bribed into being recruited as allies.

It was arranged that, at eleven o' clock at night, the bribed soldiers, including a Sergeant Ainslie, would be on guard duty at the sally port.

The attacking party would clamber up the rocks at the foot of the wall carrying a scaling ladder made of rope that would be hauled over the battlements and attached there by Ainslie, allowing

The attacking party clamber up the rocks at the foot of the wall

the attackers to take the rest of the garrison by surprise.

Once the castle was taken, three mighty discharges of artillery were to signal the success of the attempt to friends watching from the Fife shore.

A beacon fire would then be lit on the Lomond hills and, picked up from the heights of the Forfarshire hills, then signalled to the gathered clans at Invercauld. Mar and his Highlanders would then descend on the Lowlands.

But a combination of unfortunate circumstances doomed the carefully constructed plan to failure from the start: word of the scheme reached the ears of the wife of one of the plotters, who lost no time in informing the garrison commander.

Success could still have been achieved, however, if the plan had been put into effect at the agreed time of eleven o'clock.

But the raiding party had stayed too long in a nearby tavern, and by the time they were ready to storm the castle walls the garrison was alert and prepared.

In another farcical blunder, preparations for the attack were also held up because of the late arrival of the rope to fashion the necessary scaling ladder!

The ladder was at last thrown to Sergeant Ainslie

as he waited with increasing nervousness on the battlements, but it was too late.

Hearing the approach of the castle patrol he not only panicked and threw the ladder onto the rocks below, but also, in an attempt to avert suspicion from himself, fired his musket and cried 'The enemy!'

Confusion now broke out as the raiders attempted to scramble to safety, while the patrol fired down on them from the castle heights.

Of the eighty men involved in the assault, only four were captured, one of them a one-legged Jacobite veteran of the battle of Killiecrankie, and three young lads.

Mercy was shown to the four, but not to the treacherous Sergeant Ainslie, who was summarily hanged from the castle's postern gate.

The Jacobite cause received a further blow only a few weeks later after the battle of Sheriffmuir, when Mar unwisely withdrew his forces north to Perth.

Despite a brief visit to Scottish shores by the Old Pretender himself, the 1715 Rising had effectively fizzled out by the time he returned into exile in February of 1716. ✄

Defying Prince Charlie

T hirty years after the abortive Jacobite Rising of
1715, hopes of a restoration of the Royal House
of Stuart to their ancient throne were raised
once again with the arrival on Scottish shores of
Prince Charles Edward Stuart, known as the Young
Pretender, but more fondly remembered as Bonnie
Prince Charlie.

The Stuart Standard had been raised at
Glenfinnan on August 19, 1745, and by September 17
the prince was able to take the town of Edinburgh at
the head of a 3,000-strong army.

There was still one last pocket of resistance,
however, and the prince was reminded of this in no
uncertain terms when a cannonball came thundering
down what is now the present-day Royal Mile and
smashed into the walls of Holyrood Palace.

The guns of Edinburgh Castle had articulated
their defiance of the young prince and his Jacobite
army.

The Jacobites achieved a memorable victory three
days after their arrival in the town at the battle of
nearby Prestonpans, but jubilation over this was
marred by the fact that the castle was still in the
hands of their Hanoverian enemies.

With the capture or surrender of the fortress and the hoisting of the Stuart standard from its battlements, Scotland's adhesion to the Jacobite cause would be so unmistakably proclaimed that even the last waverer might be won over, but, with negotiations with the garrison proving fruitless, the prince resorted to stronger tactics.

A blockade of the castle was put into effect on September 29, and two days later the Jacobites fired on some messengers who had been attempting to smuggle supplies to the garrison.

Sporadic fire was now kept up between the garrison and the Jacobites until the castle's governor, General George Preston, warned on October 4 that he was now determined to bring his bigger guns into play unless the blockade was lifted.

The general accordingly arranged for a notice to be sent to the inhabitants of homes in the immediate neighbourhood, warning that he was about to unleash the full fire power of the castle artillery and that anyone who wanted to save their lives should do so by immediately evacuating the area.

The warning was heeded, and a steady cannonade was kept up from the castle throughout the afternoon.

Evidence of this can still be seen today, in the form of a cannon ball that has remained embedded

Despite heavy fire the Camerons stormed up to the Castle…

for more than 260 years in what is now known as Cannon Ball House, the first house on the south side of the present-day High Street and visible from the esplanade.

The garrison launched a daring assault on the Jacobite positions at the top of High Street as evening fell, managing to mount some field pieces on an earthen rampart they hastily constructed and pouring a deadly fire into the ranks of the Highlanders.

Irritated beyond endurance by this, a party of Cameron clansmen rushed the rampart and, ignoring the deadly hail of screaming metal, managed to drive the assault party back to the castle.

But the position of the Camerons was now hopelessly exposed to the artillery looking down on them from the castle's Half Moon Battery, and they had no option but to retreat back down the High Street.

Prince Charlie also found himself in a hopeless position: the abortive attempts to take the castle was costing him lives he could ill afford to lose, while the damage caused to the town by the castle guns was losing him sympathy from among its citizens.

Reluctantly, he had no option but to give the order for the blockade to be lifted.

With drums beating, pipes playing, and colours

proudly flying, the Jacobite army finally left Edinburgh on November 1 for the long march south to London.

They only reached as far as Derby, however, when the controversial decision was taken to retire back over the border.

Victory was gained at the battle of Falkirk on January 17, 1746, but Jacobite hopes were finally dashed forever in the carnage of the battle of Culloden, fought on Drummossie Moor, near Inverness, on April 16.

Edinburgh Castle played one final role in the Jacobite defeat, when the torn and bloody standards of the defeated clansmen were taken from the battlefield and displayed there for a time as spoils of war.

Further humiliation for the doomed Jacobite cause followed when the standards were burned by the public hangman at the town's Market Cross. ✂